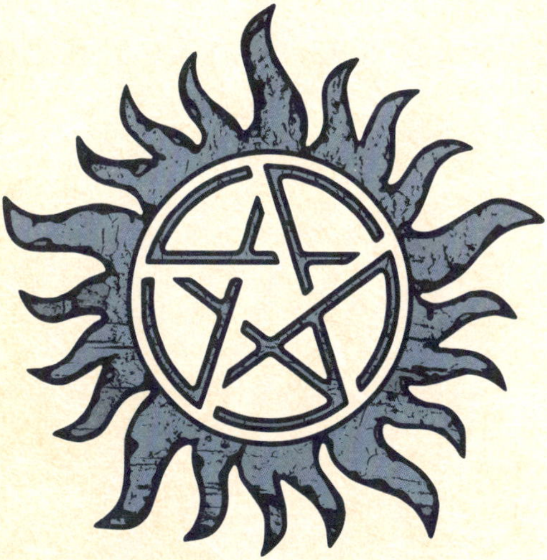

THIS BELONGS TO

DATE __/__/__

TAROT READING

MOON PHASE

Who is the tarot spread for?

QUERY

CARDS SELECTED

TAROT READING

INTERPRETATIONS

Thoughts and feelings:

DRAW YOUR SPREADS HERE

SAVING PEOPLE HUNTING THINGS THE FAMILY BUSINESS

DATE __/__/__

TAROT READING

MOON PHASE

Who is the tarot spread for?

QUERY

CARDS SELECTED

TAROT READING

INTERPRETATIONS

Thoughts and feelings:

DRAW YOUR SPREADS HERE

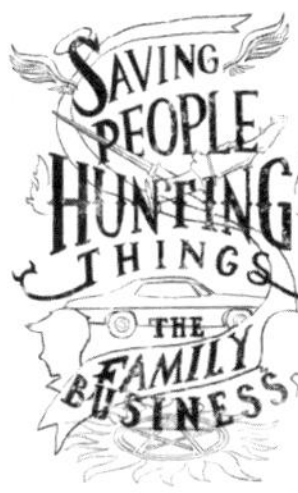
SAVING
PEOPLE
HUNTING
THINGS
THE
FAMILY
BUSINESS

DATE __/__/__

TAROT READING

MOON PHASE

Who is the tarot spread for?

QUERY

CARDS SELECTED

TAROT READING

INTERPRETATIONS

Thoughts and feelings:

DRAW YOUR SPREADS HERE

Saving People Hunting Things

The Family Business

DATE __/__/__

TAROT READING

MOON PHASE

Who is the tarot spread for?

QUERY

CARDS SELECTED

TAROT READING

INTERPRETATIONS

Thoughts and feelings:

DRAW YOUR SPREADS HERE

SAVING PEOPLE HUNTING THINGS
THE FAMILY BUSINESS

DATE __/__/__

TAROT READING

MOON PHASE

Who is the tarot spread for?

QUERY

CARDS SELECTED

TAROT READING

INTERPRETATIONS

Thoughts and feelings:

DRAW YOUR SPREADS HERE

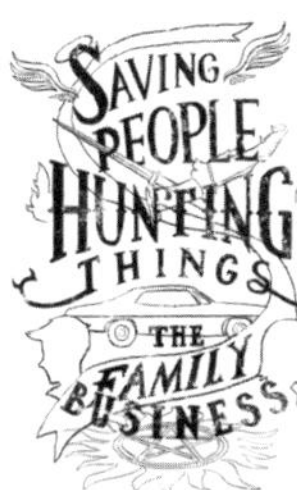
SAVING
PEOPLE
HUNTING
THINGS
THE
FAMILY
BUSINESS

DATE __/__/__

TAROT READING

MOON PHASE

Who is the tarot spread for?

QUERY

CARDS SELECTED

TAROT READING

INTERPRETATIONS

Thoughts and feelings:

DRAW YOUR SPREADS HERE

Saving People Hunting Things

The Family Business

DATE __/__/__

TAROT READING

MOON PHASE

Who is the tarot spread for?

QUERY

CARDS SELECTED

TAROT READING

INTERPRETATIONS

Thoughts and feelings:

DRAW YOUR SPREADS HERE

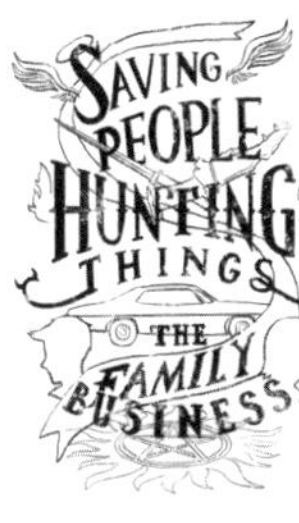
SAVING
PEOPLE
HUNTING
THINGS
THE
FAMILY
BUSINESS

DATE __/__/__

TAROT READING

MOON PHASE

Who is the tarot spread for?

QUERY

CARDS SELECTED

TAROT READING

INTERPRETATIONS

Thoughts and feelings:

DRAW YOUR SPREADS HERE

Saving People Hunting Things

The Family Business

DATE __/__/__

TAROT READING

MOON PHASE

Who is the tarot spread for?

QUERY

CARDS SELECTED

TAROT READING

INTERPRETATIONS

Thoughts and feelings:

DRAW YOUR SPREADS HERE

Saving People Hunting Things

The Family Business

DATE __/__/__

TAROT READING

MOON PHASE

Who is the tarot spread for?

QUERY

CARDS SELECTED

TAROT READING

INTERPRETATIONS

Thoughts and feelings:

DRAW YOUR SPREADS HERE

SAVING PEOPLE HUNTING THINGS THE FAMILY BUSINESS

DATE __/__/__

TAROT READING

MOON PHASE

Who is the tarot spread for?

QUERY

CARDS SELECTED

TAROT READING

INTERPRETATIONS

Thoughts and feelings:

DRAW YOUR SPREADS HERE

Saving People Hunting Things

The Family Business

DATE __/__/__

TAROT READING

MOON PHASE

Who is the tarot spread for?

QUERY

CARDS SELECTED

TAROT READING

INTERPRETATIONS

Thoughts and feelings:

DRAW YOUR SPREADS HERE

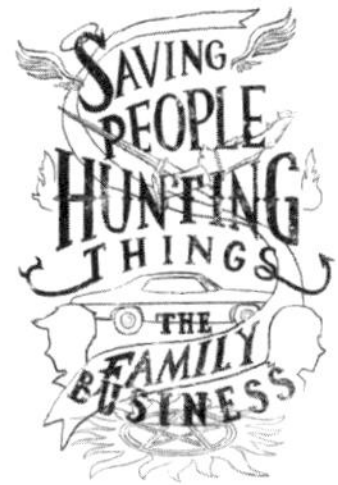
SAVING PEOPLE HUNTING THINGS
THE FAMILY BUSINESS

DATE __/__/__

TAROT READING

MOON PHASE

Who is the tarot spread for?

QUERY

CARDS SELECTED

TAROT READING

INTERPRETATIONS

Thoughts and feelings:

DRAW YOUR SPREADS HERE

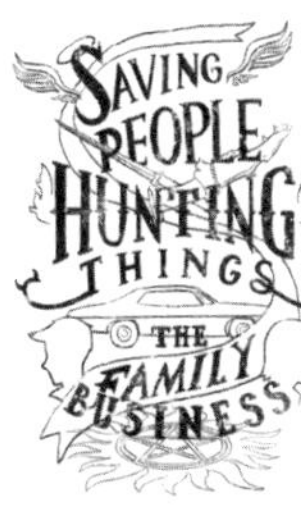
SAVING
PEOPLE
HUNTING
THINGS
THE
FAMILY
BUSINESS

DATE __/__/__

TAROT READING

MOON PHASE

Who is the tarot spread for?

QUERY

CARDS SELECTED

TAROT READING

INTERPRETATIONS

Thoughts and feelings:

DRAW YOUR SPREADS HERE

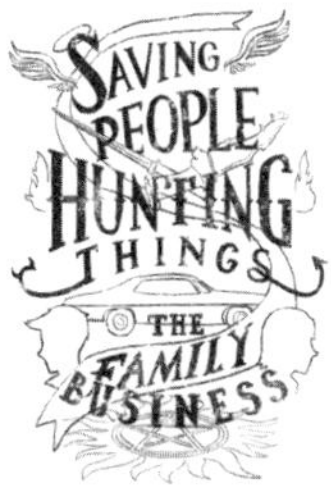
SAVING
PEOPLE
HUNTING
THINGS
THE
FAMILY
BUSINESS

DATE __/__/__

TAROT READING

MOON PHASE

Who is the tarot spread for?

QUERY

CARDS SELECTED

TAROT READING

INTERPRETATIONS

Thoughts and feelings:

DRAW YOUR SPREADS HERE

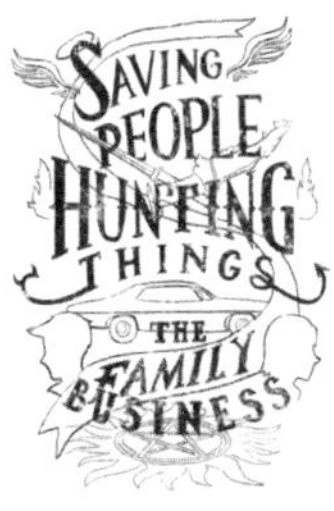
SAVING
PEOPLE
HUNTING
THINGS
THE
FAMILY
BUSINESS

DATE __/__/__

TAROT READING

MOON PHASE

Who is the tarot spread for?

QUERY

CARDS SELECTED

TAROT READING

INTERPRETATIONS

Thoughts and feelings:

DRAW YOUR SPREADS HERE

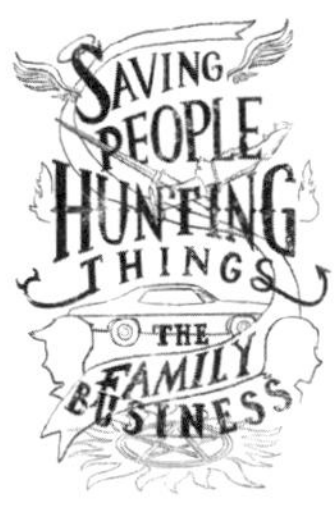
SAVING
PEOPLE
HUNTING
THINGS
THE
FAMILY
BUSINESS

DATE __/__/__

TAROT READING

MOON PHASE

Who is the tarot spread for?

QUERY

CARDS SELECTED

TAROT READING

INTERPRETATIONS

Thoughts and feelings:

DRAW YOUR SPREADS HERE

Saving People Hunting Things

The Family Business

DATE __/__/__

TAROT READING

MOON PHASE

Who is the tarot spread for?

QUERY

CARDS SELECTED

TAROT READING

INTERPRETATIONS

Thoughts and feelings:

DRAW YOUR SPREADS HERE

Saving People Hunting Things
The Family Business

DATE __/__/__

TAROT READING

MOON PHASE

Who is the tarot spread for?

QUERY

CARDS SELECTED

TAROT READING

INTERPRETATIONS

Thoughts and feelings:

DRAW YOUR SPREADS HERE

SAVING PEOPLE HUNTING THINGS

THE FAMILY BUSINESS

DATE __/__/__

TAROT READING

MOON PHASE

Who is the tarot spread for?

QUERY

CARDS SELECTED

TAROT READING

INTERPRETATIONS

Thoughts and feelings:

DRAW YOUR SPREADS HERE

Saving People Hunting Things
The Family Business

DATE __/__/__

TAROT READING

MOON PHASE

Who is the tarot spread for?

QUERY

CARDS SELECTED

TAROT READING

INTERPRETATIONS

Thoughts and feelings:

DRAW YOUR SPREADS HERE

SAVING PEOPLE HUNTING THINGS

THE FAMILY BUSINESS

DATE __/__/__

TAROT READING

MOON PHASE

Who is the tarot spread for?

QUERY

CARDS SELECTED

TAROT READING

INTERPRETATIONS

Thoughts and feelings:

DRAW YOUR SPREADS HERE

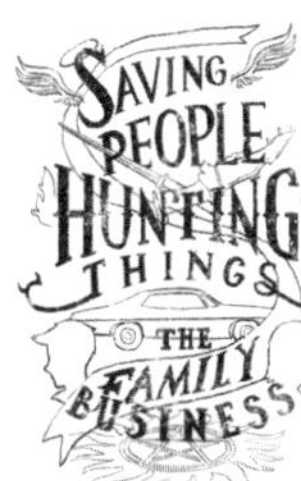
SAVING
PEOPLE
HUNTING
THINGS
THE
FAMILY
BUSINESS

DATE __/__/__

TAROT READING

MOON PHASE

Who is the tarot spread for?

QUERY

CARDS SELECTED

TAROT READING

INTERPRETATIONS

Thoughts and feelings:

DRAW YOUR SPREADS HERE

Saving People Hunting Things
The Family Business

DATE __/__/__

TAROT READING

MOON PHASE

Who is the tarot spread for?

QUERY

CARDS SELECTED

TAROT READING

INTERPRETATIONS

Thoughts and feelings:

DRAW YOUR SPREADS HERE

SAVING PEOPLE HUNTING THINGS THE FAMILY BUSINESS

DATE __/__/__

TAROT READING

MOON PHASE

Who is the tarot spread for?

QUERY

CARDS SELECTED

TAROT READING

INTERPRETATIONS

Thoughts and feelings:

DRAW YOUR SPREADS HERE

SAVING PEOPLE HUNTING THINGS

THE FAMILY BUSINESS

DATE __/__/__

TAROT READING

MOON PHASE

Who is the tarot spread for?

QUERY

CARDS SELECTED

TAROT READING

INTERPRETATIONS

Thoughts and feelings:

DRAW YOUR SPREADS HERE

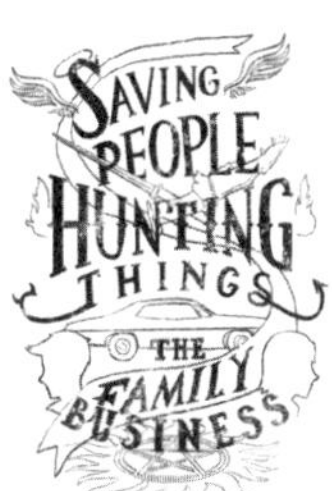
SAVING
PEOPLE
HUNTING
THINGS
THE
FAMILY
BUSINESS

DATE __/__/__

TAROT READING

MOON PHASE

Who is the tarot spread for?

QUERY

CARDS SELECTED

TAROT READING

INTERPRETATIONS

Thoughts and feelings:

DRAW YOUR SPREADS HERE

Saving People Hunting Things

The Family Business

DATE __/__/__

TAROT READING

MOON PHASE

Who is the tarot spread for?

QUERY

CARDS SELECTED

TAROT READING

INTERPRETATIONS

Thoughts and feelings:

DRAW YOUR SPREADS HERE

Saving People Hunting Things The Family Business

DATE __/__/__

TAROT READING

MOON PHASE

Who is the tarot spread for?

QUERY

CARDS SELECTED

TAROT READING

INTERPRETATIONS

Thoughts and feelings:

DRAW YOUR SPREADS HERE

SAVING PEOPLE HUNTING THINGS THE FAMILY BUSINESS

DATE __/__/__

TAROT READING

MOON PHASE

Who is the tarot spread for?

QUERY

CARDS SELECTED

TAROT READING

INTERPRETATIONS

Thoughts and feelings:

DRAW YOUR SPREADS HERE

Saving People Hunting Things

The Family Business

DATE __/__/__

TAROT READING

MOON PHASE

Who is the tarot spread for?

QUERY

CARDS SELECTED

TAROT READING

INTERPRETATIONS

Thoughts and feelings:

DRAW YOUR SPREADS HERE

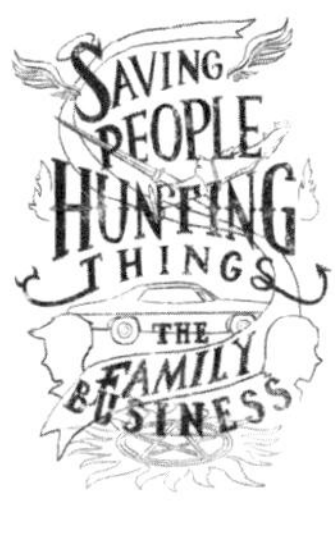
SAVING
PEOPLE
HUNTING
THINGS
THE
FAMILY
BUSINESS

DATE __/__/__

TAROT READING

MOON PHASE

Who is the tarot spread for?

QUERY

CARDS SELECTED

TAROT READING

INTERPRETATIONS

Thoughts and feelings:

DRAW YOUR SPREADS HERE

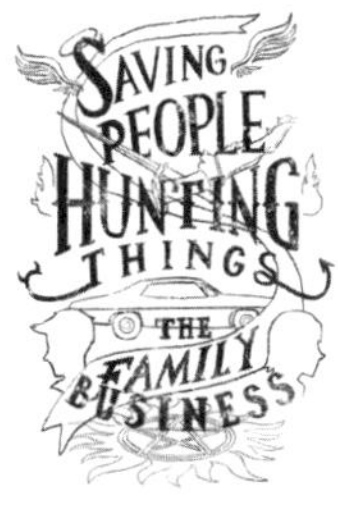
SAVING
PEOPLE
HUNTING
THINGS
THE
FAMILY
BUSINESS

DATE __/__/__

TAROT READING

MOON PHASE

Who is the tarot spread for?

QUERY

CARDS SELECTED

TAROT READING

INTERPRETATIONS

Thoughts and feelings:

DRAW YOUR SPREADS HERE

Saving People
Hunting Things
The Family Business

DATE __/__/__

TAROT READING

MOON PHASE

Who is the tarot spread for?

QUERY

CARDS SELECTED

TAROT READING

INTERPRETATIONS

Thoughts and feelings:

DRAW YOUR SPREADS HERE

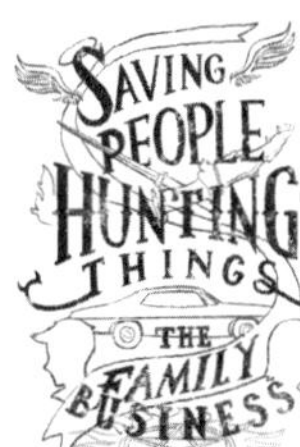
SAVING
PEOPLE
HUNTING
THINGS
THE
FAMILY
BUSINESS

DATE __/__/__

TAROT READING

MOON PHASE

Who is the tarot spread for?

QUERY

CARDS SELECTED

TAROT READING

INTERPRETATIONS

Thoughts and feelings:

DRAW YOUR SPREADS HERE

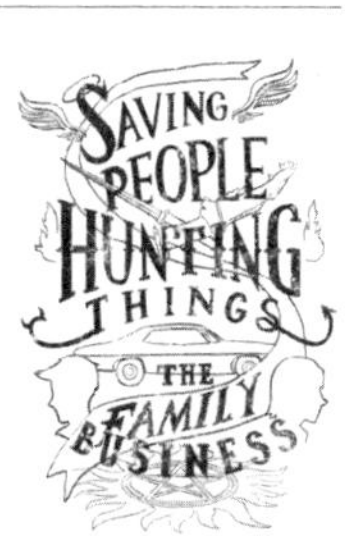
SAVING
PEOPLE
HUNTING
THINGS
THE
FAMILY
BUSINESS

DATE __/__/__

TAROT READING

MOON PHASE

Who is the tarot spread for?

QUERY

CARDS SELECTED

TAROT READING

INTERPRETATIONS

Thoughts and feelings:

DRAW YOUR SPREADS HERE

Saving People Hunting Things

The Family Business

DATE __/__/__

TAROT READING

MOON PHASE

Who is the tarot spread for?

QUERY

CARDS SELECTED

TAROT READING

INTERPRETATIONS

Thoughts and feelings:

DRAW YOUR SPREADS HERE

Saving People Hunting Things

The Family Business

DATE __/__/__

TAROT READING

MOON PHASE

Who is the tarot spread for?

QUERY

CARDS SELECTED

TAROT READING

INTERPRETATIONS

Thoughts and feelings:

DRAW YOUR SPREADS HERE

Saving People Hunting Things

The Family Business

DATE __/__/__

TAROT READING

MOON PHASE

Who is the tarot spread for?

QUERY

CARDS SELECTED

TAROT READING

INTERPRETATIONS

Thoughts and feelings:

DRAW YOUR SPREADS HERE

SAVING PEOPLE HUNTING THINGS

THE FAMILY BUSINESS

DATE __/__/__

TAROT READING

MOON PHASE

Who is the tarot spread for?

QUERY

CARDS SELECTED

TAROT READING

INTERPRETATIONS

Thoughts and feelings:

DRAW YOUR SPREADS HERE

SAVING PEOPLE HUNTING THINGS

THE FAMILY BUSINESS

DATE __/__/__

TAROT READING

MOON PHASE

Who is the tarot spread for?

QUERY

CARDS SELECTED

TAROT READING

INTERPRETATIONS

Thoughts and feelings:

DRAW YOUR SPREADS HERE

Saving People Hunting Things

The Family Business

DATE __/__/__

TAROT READING

MOON PHASE

Who is the tarot spread for?

QUERY

CARDS SELECTED

TAROT READING

INTERPRETATIONS

Thoughts and feelings:

DRAW YOUR SPREADS HERE

SAVING PEOPLE HUNTING THINGS THE FAMILY BUSINESS

DATE __/__/__

TAROT READING

MOON PHASE

Who is the tarot spread for?

QUERY

CARDS SELECTED

TAROT READING

INTERPRETATIONS

Thoughts and feelings:

DRAW YOUR SPREADS HERE

Saving People Hunting Things

The Family Business

DATE __/__/__

TAROT READING

MOON PHASE

Who is the tarot spread for?

QUERY

CARDS SELECTED

TAROT READING

INTERPRETATIONS

Thoughts and feelings:

DRAW YOUR SPREADS HERE

Saving People Hunting Things

The Family Business

DATE __/__/__

TAROT READING

MOON PHASE

Who is the tarot spread for?

QUERY

CARDS SELECTED

TAROT READING

INTERPRETATIONS

Thoughts and feelings:

DRAW YOUR SPREADS HERE

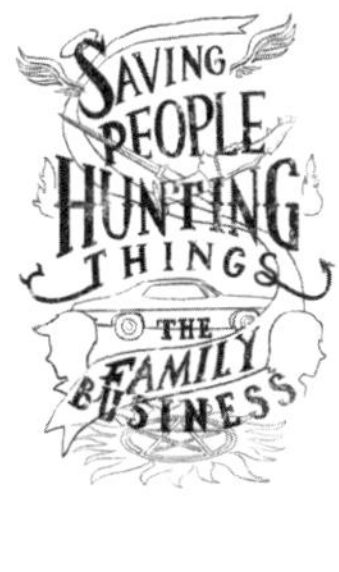
Saving
People
Hunting
Things
The
Family
Business

DATE __/__/__

TAROT READING

MOON PHASE

Who is the tarot spread for?

QUERY

CARDS SELECTED

TAROT READING

INTERPRETATIONS

Thoughts and feelings:

DRAW YOUR SPREADS HERE

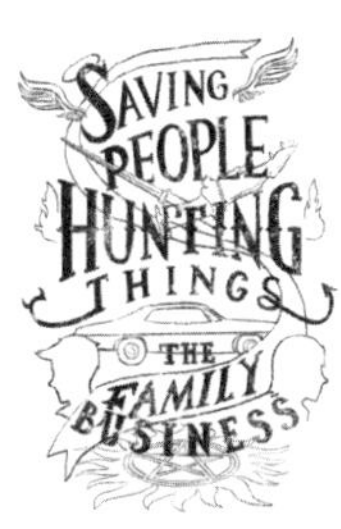
SAVING
PEOPLE
HUNTING
THINGS
THE
FAMILY
BUSINESS

DATE __/__/__

TAROT READING

MOON PHASE

Who is the tarot spread for?

QUERY

CARDS SELECTED

TAROT READING

INTERPRETATIONS

Thoughts and feelings:

DRAW YOUR SPREADS HERE

Saving People Hunting Things

The Family Business

DATE __/__/__

TAROT READING

MOON PHASE

Who is the tarot spread for?

QUERY

CARDS SELECTED

TAROT READING

INTERPRETATIONS

Thoughts and feelings:

DRAW YOUR SPREADS HERE

Looking at the Renaissance